CHRISTMAS in all the world

Stories about Christmas customs in 40 nations.

85 figures to cut out, inspired by the folklore of five continents, by Francois Craenhals.

AUGSBURG Publishing House • Minneapolis

Contents

CHRISTMAS IN ALL THE WORLD

1979 First United States of America Edition
Augsburg Publishing House

English text by Carolynne and Gordon Lathrop

Library of Congress Catalog Card No. 79-50087

International Standard Book No. 0-8066-1704-7

Manufactured in Belgium

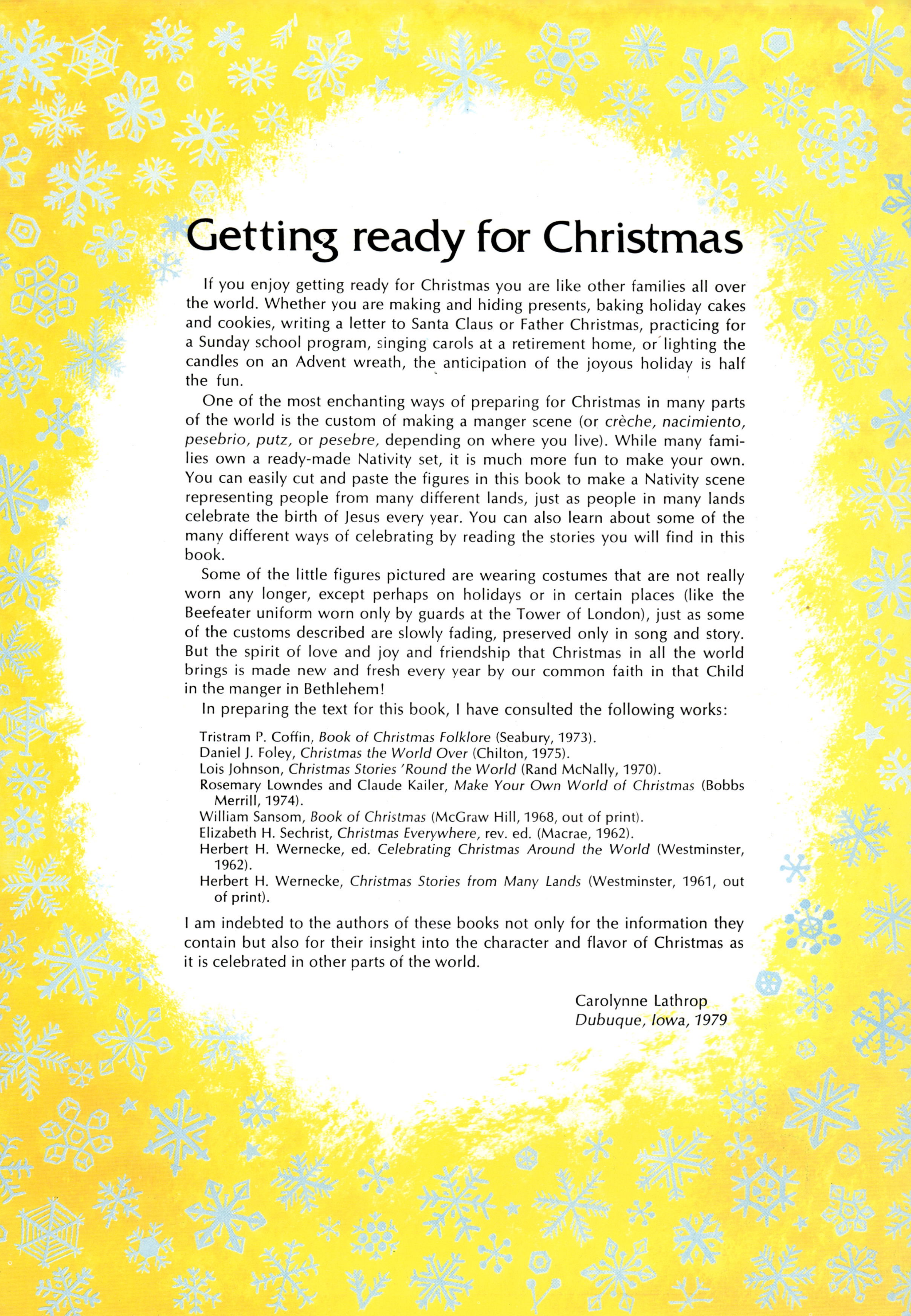

Getting ready for Christmas

If you enjoy getting ready for Christmas you are like other families all over the world. Whether you are making and hiding presents, baking holiday cakes and cookies, writing a letter to Santa Claus or Father Christmas, practicing for a Sunday school program, singing carols at a retirement home, or lighting the candles on an Advent wreath, the anticipation of the joyous holiday is half the fun.

One of the most enchanting ways of preparing for Christmas in many parts of the world is the custom of making a manger scene (or *crèche, nacimiento, pesebrio, putz,* or *pesebre,* depending on where you live). While many families own a ready-made Nativity set, it is much more fun to make your own. You can easily cut and paste the figures in this book to make a Nativity scene representing people from many different lands, just as people in many lands celebrate the birth of Jesus every year. You can also learn about some of the many different ways of celebrating by reading the stories you will find in this book.

Some of the little figures pictured are wearing costumes that are not really worn any longer, except perhaps on holidays or in certain places (like the Beefeater uniform worn only by guards at the Tower of London), just as some of the customs described are slowly fading, preserved only in song and story. But the spirit of love and joy and friendship that Christmas in all the world brings is made new and fresh every year by our common faith in that Child in the manger in Bethlehem!

In preparing the text for this book, I have consulted the following works:

Tristram P. Coffin, *Book of Christmas Folklore* (Seabury, 1973).

Daniel J. Foley, *Christmas the World Over* (Chilton, 1975).

Lois Johnson, *Christmas Stories 'Round the World* (Rand McNally, 1970).

Rosemary Lowndes and Claude Kailer, *Make Your Own World of Christmas* (Bobbs Merrill, 1974).

William Sansom, *Book of Christmas* (McGraw Hill, 1968, out of print).

Elizabeth H. Sechrist, *Christmas Everywhere*, rev. ed. (Macrae, 1962).

Herbert H. Wernecke, ed. *Celebrating Christmas Around the World* (Westminster, 1962).

Herbert H. Wernecke, *Christmas Stories from Many Lands* (Westminster, 1961, out of print).

I am indebted to the authors of these books not only for the information they contain but also for their insight into the character and flavor of Christmas as it is celebrated in other parts of the world.

Carolynne Lathrop
Dubuque, Iowa, 1979

Instructions

1

2
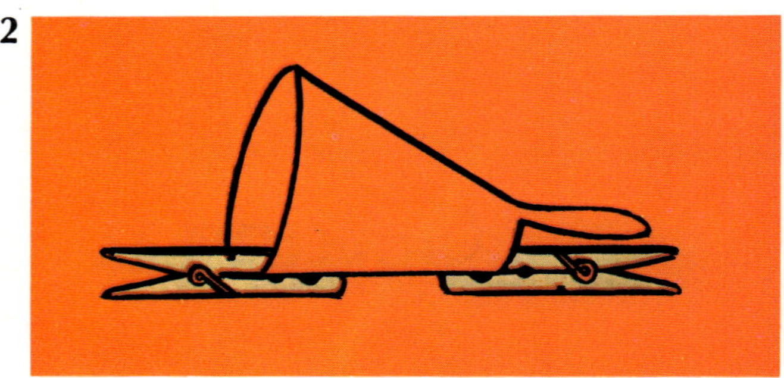

1. Cut out each figure and spread the white strip with glue.
2. Fold into a cone, with the glued strip and the wrong side of the figure together. Clip with spring-type clothes pins. Allow to dry.

3. Cut out the legs and spread one end with glue.
4. Fold into a cylinder, with the glue against the center back of the leg piece.

3
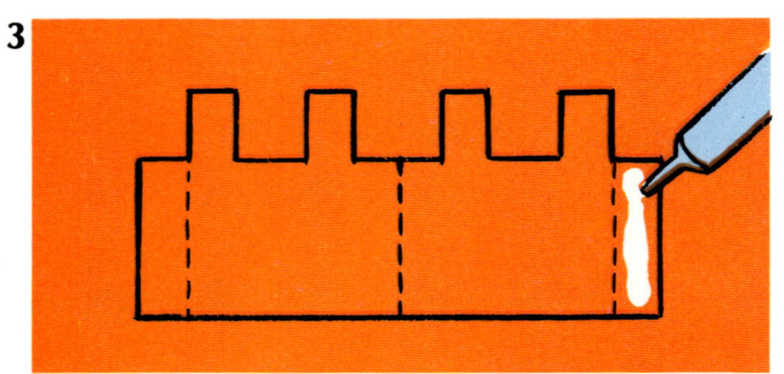

4
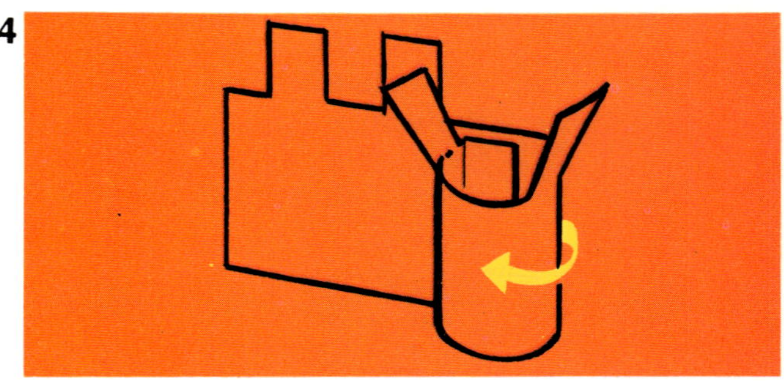

5

6

5. Clip with clothes pin. Glue the other end in the same way.
6. Gently separate the legs a little by rotating them, and allow to dry.

7. Fold back the four tabs at the top of the legs. Spread with glue.
8. Glue footpiece in place inside cone. Stick arms, hats, etc. on figure where needed.

7
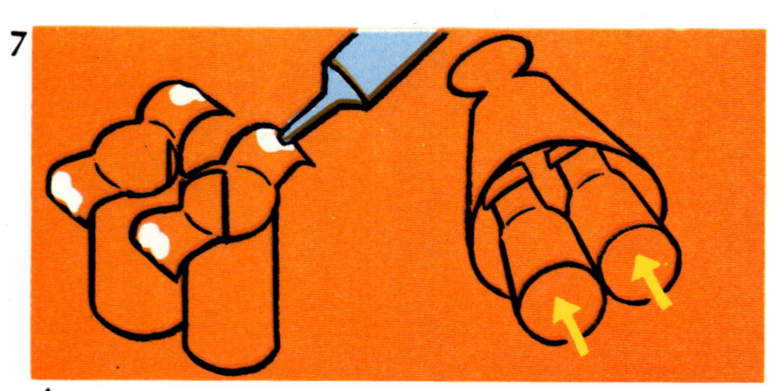

8

Joseph
Jesus
Mary

Belgium

For Belgian children, the holiday season begins early. Boys and girls wake on December 6 to find that St. Nicholas has stuffed their shoes with candy and toys.

Christmas is primarily a religious holiday in Belgium. In some towns costumed children form processions on their way to church. One boy dresses as St. John the Baptist, carrying a cross and leading a lamb, both symbols of Christ.

In a pageant known as *Bethlehem,* children have long acted out the Christmas story in Flanders, the Dutch-speaking part of Belgium. In Walonia, where French is spoken, marionettes are used to tell the story. This still occurs in the *Bethlehem* of Verviers.

Once this was an outdoor marionette show with many scenes. The people moved from one elaborate setting to another, and an old woman told the traditional story which she had learned from her mother. Now it is given in the local museum and the text is recorded. Only the story of the birth of Christ remains the same!

Germany

In many German homes the first sign of the approaching holy day is the Advent wreath which appears four weeks before Christmas. This is usually a circle of greenery with four candles, one to be lighted the first Sunday in Advent, two to be lighted the second Sunday, and so on until all four burn brightly. Advent is a time of preparation for the coming feast, and from German kitchens drift the spicy fragrances of lebkuchen, springerle, and other traditional breads and cookies.

Some towns feature Christmas fairs, like the Christkindl Markt in Nuremberg, where countless toys and ornaments are displayed and purchased. In many families it is the Christ child himself who sends gifts to the children by way of the "Christkindl angel," a child dressed up in white with a filmy veil and perhaps even golden wings. If this mysterious messenger does not appear herself, a pile of gifts may suddenly appear near an open window.

Tradition has it that Christmas trees began in Germany. Our fragile glass baubles now replace the apples and paper roses with which the trees were originally hung. One legend suggests that Martin Luther decorated the very first Christmas tree for his children. He explained that the glowing candles symbolized Christ, the Light of the World.

Melchior
Balthasar
Caspar

India

Just as in many other faraway lands, people in India have learned about Christmas from European missionaries, especially the English. Because most of India's people are not Christian, Christmas Day is not a national holiday. But there are Christian congregations which celebrate Christmas much as we do. The people go to church very early on Christmas morning for a service that lasts until daybreak. They sing hymns they have written for the holiday.

Gifts may be exchanged and parties held in the missions. The Christmas trees may be banana trees still adorned with growing bananas. Poinsettia trees provide a more traditional decoration. A typical gift might be a lemon, symbolizing the giver's wishes for good fortune and a long life.

Haiti

In the church of St. Martin in Port-au-Prince Christmas means, above all, making music. For weeks on end the songs for the Christmas Eve mass are practiced. At last the festive evening arrives. By eight o'clock there is already a long line in front of the door. Everyone wants to be sure of a seat in the church! At eleven o'clock the doors finally open.

Noel, Noel, Noel! Plein minuit non sava nana,
Youn lumière sort nan ciel nan pays Bethléem.

In this old French dialect of the country, where many races and nationalities have been joined, joy is conveyed through very soft singing:

Christmas, Christmas, Christmas! It is midnight throughout the land.
A light comes from heaven to Bethlehem-country.

The drowsy rhythms of these songs continue during the entire service until everyone is outside again.

"Noel a la Caye" follows, including feasting, wearing new clothes, and dancing until the following morning to the sounds of drums, trombones, castanets, and the people of Port-au-Prince.

Morocco
Sweden
Japan
Cambodia

Bulgaria

For Christians in Bulgaria, midnight mass is central to Christmas Eve celebrations. Christmas Eve supper may be simply fruit soup and bread with a coin baked inside—bringing good luck to its finder. After the people have stood during the lengthy Orthodox service, they may break their 40-day fast with a roasted sparrow, caught in the wheat field where it had fed. Besides its connection with the earth and the grain, the sparrow is said to bring music to the soul of the person who eats it.

Other customs also show ties with centuries of farming in Bulgaria. In some households the father puts a handful of wheat, along with a coin, into a sock and hangs it on a tree for the birds to eat while the family enjoys a hearty Christmas dinner. Then he lays a few kernels of grain on the threshold, and announces to his family "Christ is born," and they respond "He is born indeed."

In another custom the father takes the bellows from the fireplace and pumps air into the faces of each person in the family, wishing each one good health.

Czechoslovakia

Although children in Czechoslovakia expect St. Nicholas, accompanied by a devil named Cert, to bring them toys on "Svaty Mikales" Day, December 6, the whole family celebrates Christmas for three days, December 24-26. Stuffed and baked carp is a popular dish on these feast days.

Hand-crafted *jeslicky,* or manger scenes, have long been traditional in many Czech homes. Most figures have been carved by family members from wood or molded from bread dough, and are painted with bright colors. Christmas trees are a more recent custom, but the decorations have been developed into a real art. Farm families have always made their own tree-trimmings from natural materials: apples, prunes, nuts, pastries and gingerbread, wood and straw, and colorful scraps of paper and fabric.

Many Czech carols, or *koledy,* are sung in that country, but the Czech legend we know best was made popular in an English carol. Everyone has heard of Wenceslas, a 10th century prince of Bohemia (now part of Czechoslovakia). He devoted his life to promoting the spread of Christianity until he was killed on his way to church by his ambitious brother Boleslas. The legend made familiar in the 19th century hymn "Good King Wenceslas" tells how on St. Stephen's Day (December 26) he took food to a poor peasant freezing in the cold. The warmth of his Christian love cast a glow that melted the snow.

Poland
United States
Vietnam
Norway

Taiwan and China

The most important winter holiday in Taiwan is the Chinese New Year. In late January or early February, depending on the position of the moon, there is a week-long celebration. It begins with offerings made to heaven and earth as family members and ancestors are honored, and includes feasting, gift giving, and fireworks. Everyone saves his or her money for new clothes or at least a lantern for the spectacular Feast of the Lanterns.

A small number, about one percent, of people on the island of Taiwan, and perhaps in the People's Republic of China as well, are Christian. For them Christmas (*Sheng Dan Jieh,* or "Holy Birth Festival") is also a great feast. Children may hang up bulky muslin stockings, large enough for the toys to be brought by *Lan Khoong-Khoong* ("Nice Old Father"). Costly gifts are exchanged only by family members, while friends and distant relatives are given gifts of flowers or food. Paper lanterns, chains, and flowers decorate homes and churches, which may also contain brightly-trimmed Christmas trees, called "Trees of Light."

Sri Lanka

The Christians in Ceylon celebrate Christmas with church services, carols, and family feasts and visits. In Kandy, Christmas Eve may be heralded with fireworks, dancing, and the beating of drums, and further lighted with lanterns, torches, and huge bonfires.

One resident told of a rural Christian town that built a miniature village on a vacant lot. The home and way of life of each of the 60 families in town was represented. The local church served a delicious meal prepared by the young people so that everyone could celebrate the holiday together.

India
Turkey
Laos
Burma

Cuba

In Cuba Christmas and Epiphany are still important holidays. Many families construct elaborate Nativity scenes. Besides the traditional stable, these include models of local schools, homes, and other buildings, landscaped gardens and farms, forests and brooks, and even family pets. Often these scenes are set up in front of the house or in the courtyard or garden, so that passersby may see and enjoy the family's handiwork.

Children in Cuba receive their gifts on January 6, Epiphany, when they are delivered by the "Three Kings." Sometimes all the gifts for the children of a particular school or church may be collected and given out by three schoolboys. Dressed in royal-looking costumes, they solemnly deliver the presents from door to door.

Poland

A variety of customs help Polish people celebrate Christmas. Children may receive gifts from St. Nicholas on December 6. Early on Christmas Eve, they may also leave a letter on the windowsill for the "Mother Star" or the "Three Wise Men" to find as they deliver gifts later that evening.

The appearance of the first star on Christmas Eve marks the end of the Advent fast and the beginning of the Christmas feast or the "Festival of the Star" in Poland. A few wisps of straw are laid under the table and beneath the tablecloth, a reminder of the stable at Bethlehem. *Oplatki,* thin white wafers stamped with a Nativity scene, are broken and shared by all the family. This custom stems from the breaking of the bread in the mass. A place is set and kept vacant for the Christ child, whose spirit is believed to be with them. The meal might include borscht, pike with saffron or carp with prunes or raisins, noodles with poppy seeds, dumplings with sauerkraut and mushrooms, and a variety of desserts.

After dinner the children may be asked questions by the "Star Man," probably a local priest in appropriate costume. If they answer correctly they are rewarded with small gifts from the Star Man or from the Three Wise Men (or "Star Boys," as they are sometimes known—young boys of the village who accompany him).

During the week after Christmas, *joselki* (small movable puppet theaters or "peep shows") feature manger scenes or episodes from Jesus' life. A colorful scene of buildings or towers called a *szopka* provides a backdrop for the popular shows, derived from old miracle and mystery plays.

Belgium
Mexico

England

In most English homes the twelve days of Christmas have been condensed into one or two, but many old traditions are still important. Few families have fireplaces large enough to burn the traditional yule log, keeping the unburned fragments as kindling for the next year's log. The children may use the fireplace, however, to send letters up the chimney to Father Christmas, the British version of Santa Claus, and may hang their stockings there. But most stockings or pillowcases are hung on the children's bedposts, where (fat and lumpy with surprises) they are what each child first sees on Christmas morning.

The crowned boar's head with an orange in its mouth, customary in medieval England, has been replaced by turkey with chestnut stuffing or roast goose or other animal. Flaming plum pudding, bristling with currants and raisins (not plums!), rich with suet, eggs, and spices, and trimmed with a sprig of holly, is part of most Christmas menus. Extra puddings may be prepared and kept in the pantry for birthdays and other holidays. Also traditional are little mince pies and Christmas cake, a dark fruitcake frosted with marzipan.

Most English homes boast a bauble-trimmed Christmas tree. Garlands of evergreens, bunches of holly and ivy, and sprigs of mistletoe also decorate many homes. A Victorian custom still popular is the exchanging of Christmas cards.

Carol-singing is popular in many places, and services of lessons and carols are favorites on Christmas Eve. Some lucky children are treated to a Christmas afternoon pantomime or puppet show, perhaps Punch and Judy or a familiar fairy tale, before going home for a Christmas tea. Festivities continue on Boxing Day, December 26, once the day when boxes of goodies were given to servants and tradesmen.

Italy

Shortly before Christmas *presepi,* or manger scenes, begin to appear in nearly every home and shop in Italy. These are sometimes elaborate works of art or simple groups of clay figures. A *presepio* might be a crèche carved of butter against towers of canned goods in a grocery store, or an abundance of marzipan figures in a bake shop.

In some parts of the country *zampognari* (bagpipers) or *pifferari* (minstrels) come down from the mountains to the city on Christmas Eve to play variations of shepherd tunes on their pipes or cellos or violins. Except for the hymns sung at midnight mass, these tunes take the place of Christmas carols in Italy.

Some family gifts may be given to children by *Gesu Bambino,* the Christ child, but the children receive most of their presents on January 6 from *La Befana* (a name derived from the Italian word for Epiphany). According to tradition *La Befana* was an old woman who was told to follow the star to Bethlehem. Because she swept her house first, she missed seeing the star and lost her way. Since then, every Epiphany she rides her broomstick throughout the sky, seeking the holy family, rewarding good children by dropping sweets and presents down the chimneys, and punishing naughty ones with switches and pieces of coal.

Argentina
Peru
France
India

Guatemala

Before Christmas actually begins, Guatemalans celebrate El Dia de Guadelupe on December 8, honoring the Virgin of Guadelupe. All the children dress up in traditional Indian costumes and participate in the fiesta and parade. Grown-ups have their own parade at night.

Most Guatemalan families have a *nacimiento* at Christmas time. This is a small platform on which small figures of men and women are arranged around a cradle. Often this is adorned with pine branches and brightly colored toy birds and other animals.

Nine days before Christmas friends gather for the first *posada*. A man carries statues of Mary and Joseph through the dark street. The people carry *farolitos* (painted tin lanterns) and walk to the special rhythm of a tortoiseshell drum heard only at the Christmas *posadas*.

When they reach a friend's home they sing a carol, asking the housekeeper for a place to stay. The family pretends to refuse them, then finally admits them and places the figures of Mary and Joseph in the prepared *nacimiento*. The guests and hosts have a brief devotional service and enjoy refreshments, tamales, hot punch, and almond cake. The following eight evenings the *posada* is repeated, with the figures being carried to a different home each night until Christmas Eve, when the last family invites everyone to a party. Then the Christ child is added to the *nacimiento*. Often each child has his own little figure, because each loves the Babe so much.

Australia

Because most Australians are of British descent, they keep some of the English customs. But since Australia is in the Southern Hemisphere, Christmas there falls in the height of the summer. The plum pudding and fruitcake and the roaring yule logs of England do not seem as appropriate in Australia's hot, dry climate.

In some cities, hundreds of people gather on Christmas Eve for carol singing by candlelight. The next day families exchange gifts and may spend part of Christmas or the day after—called "Boxing Day"—at the beach with a picnic supper.

Tahiti
Kenya
Bulgaria
Bulgaria

The Holy Land

At Christmas time, many tourists and religious pilgrims flock to the town of Bethlehem, where Jesus was born. Christmas is a time for worship and family gatherings in Bethlehem. The Roman Patriarch of Jerusalem leads a stately Christmas Eve procession to the enormous Church of the Nativity, where five masses take place in different parts of the church. Some western visitors prefer a brief service of lessons and carols held on the Field of the Shepherds outside the town. Members of the Greek Orthodox Church, with the Copts and Syrians, have a similar procession and mass on January 6, which is Christmas according to an older calendar. Members of the Armenian church celebrate on Epiphany, January 18 in the older calendar.

Whatever the date, the spirit of reverence and joy which fills the hearts of all Christians as they remember Jesus' birth brings a moment of happiness to a town surrounded by strife and hostility.

Netherlands

Children in the Netherlands spend the days before December 5, *Sinterklaasavond* (St. Nicholas' Eve), in gleeful preparations and joyous suspense. Every bake shop displays clever marzipan figures (huge pigs, great sausages, fruits and vegetables), *banket* letters (flaky pastry filled with almond paste), large, old-fashioned-looking *taai poppen* (tough dolls) made of chewy gingerbread and thin, crisp, *speculaas* hearts.

Everyone finds original and amusing ways to wrap gifts to be exchanged on *Sinterklaasavond.* Small trinkets may be hidden in a lump of clay, in a bowl of pudding, or disguised by false labels or placement in a series of boxes. Presents are accompanied by humorous verses, gently teasing the receiver.

St. Nicholas, called *Sinterklaas,* has already arrived in Holland on a big boat from Spain. Dressed in his bishop's robe and mitre, he is accompanied by *Zwarte Piet,* a young Moorish boy (younger at least than *Sinterklaas,* whose age is reckoned at about 1400 years!). He rides a white horse from roof to roof and fills children's shoes with goodies. Naughty children (rarely seen in the Netherlands in the weeks before December 5!) are punished with lumps of coal.

December 25 is a religious holiday and family feast, spent quietly at church and at home, and a special Christmas dinner is served. December 26, "Second Christmas Day," is spent in a similar way. Most Dutch homes have Christmas trees decorated with glass balls and figures of mushrooms, and sparkling with red and white lights.

Saudi Arabia
Guadeloupe
United States
United States

Chile

Christmas in Chile is chiefly a religious festival, especially in parts of the country where there are many poor people. But many Chileans make a Christmas pilgrimage to the Shrine of the Virgin del Rosario in Andacolla, a wooden statue whose hiding place is said to have been miraculously revealed to a native Indian. The town conducts a procession and special ceremonies, as well as a Christmas *fiesta* with horse races, stalls displaying native crafts, and Indian dancers in colorful costumes. Chileans enjoy *pan de pasqua,* Christmas bread filled with candied fruit, and *azuela de ave,* chicken soup containing corn on the cob and other vegetables. Children hope for gifts from *Viejo Pascuero,* "Old Christmas Man," who travels through the air with his reindeer and comes through a window only after they are asleep.

Yugoslavia

One of Yugoslavia's oldest traditions is that of the yule log, or *badnyak.* The tree is cut in a special ceremony early on Christmas Eve. Only one end of the log is placed in the fireplace, so that it will burn for many days. Wheat and wine are sprinkled on the log to ensure a prosperous year.

Before supper, straw is strewn on the floor of the house, to remind the family of the stable. The father stands by the hearth and throws walnuts into each of the four corners of the room to symbolize the Christmas spirit reaching around the world in all directions. Then they are found and eaten by the children.

The family greets each other with "Christ is born" and "He is born indeed" instead of saying "Merry Christmas." Christmas Eve supper is usually soup, fish, and noodles with chestnuts and prunes. On Christmas Day, a roast pig and stuffed whole cabbage are traditional. There is a special Christmas cake called a *chesnitsa,* which always contains the first cup of water drawn on Christmas morning, and a silver coin to bring good luck.

Indonesia
Mexico
Algeria
India

Mexico

Mexican people begin celebrating Christmas with their first *posada* (inn), nine days before Christmas. The procession of friends and neighbors enacting Mary and Joseph's search for a place to stay is turned away from eight different homes during the first eight nights. On the ninth evening, those in the procession (singing carols and carrying torches or candles) are finally admitted to a home, where they celebrate with refreshments and music. Or a single family may have its own *posada,* knocking on the door of each room of its house in turn.

Most families have *nacimientos* or crèches, where the figure of the Christ child is laid on Christmas Eve. After the *posadas,* children frequently enjoy a *pinata* party. The *pinata* is a large hollow animal, fish, bird, or other figure made from earthenware or papier-maché and brightly decorated with crepe paper or tinsel. It is filled with candy, nuts, and small toys and trinkets. The children, blindfolded, take turns trying to break it with a stick so that everyone can happily scramble for the surprises. In some places there are three *pinatas,* one filled with treats, the others with water and confetti. Each child hits at a *pinata,* hoping to break it and be covered with candy and presents, not water or confetti.

Indian stalls called *puestos* display for several weeks before Christmas a wealth of handmade toys, baskets, blankets, candies, cheese, home-grown hot peppers, and other colorful wares. But most Mexican children have to wait to receive their presents until the *Reyes Magos,* the Wise Men, fill their shoes on January 6!

Martinique

Macouba is a village on the northern end of Martinique, an island in the French Antilles. The Christmas customs in Martinique are very different from those in France itself.

In Macouba, just as everywhere on the island, a pig is slaughtered for the Christmas feast. For a whole year it has been fattened. Between the courses of the feast there is loud singing. Often the people sing very old Creole songs which, strangely enough, make fun of themselves and their customs.

Lebanon
Dahomey
Cameroon
China

American Colonies

The Puritan Christmas observed by the Pilgrims in 17th century New England was purely a time for worship and quiet, with no feasting, music, and revelry, at least not openly. Other settlers brought different customs to Virginia, where Christmas became a joyous celebration. Bringing in the yule log, drinking toasts from the wassail bowl, singing Christmas carols, and preparing gingerbread, mince pies, and elaborate Christmas dinners were enjoyed by colonial Virginians.

Moravians coming from Germany to Bethlehem, Pennsylvania, brought their own traditions. Instrumental and vocal music were important in their church services. The people dipped candles of pure beeswax to symbolize the Light of the World. Cinnamon stars, angel sugar cookies, hearts, and figures made of gingerbread were a few of the many shapes and kinds of cookies baked there. The focal point of the Moravian home was the *putz,* elaborately constructed and revealed to the children after the Christmas Eve service. The *putz* was the Moravian version of a manger scene, in which wooden figures were grouped under a Christmas tree, with moss as a base. Tiny fences and gnarled stumps were preserved from year to year. Sand, little plants, rocks, water, and other simple materials were fashioned into a cave landscaped with miniature ponds, trees, and flowers.

In New Amsterdam (New York), children of Dutch settlers happily put out their shoes on December 5 for St. Nikolaas to fill with candy and toys. They affectionately called the good bishop *Sinterklaas,* which soon became *Santy Claus* or Santa Claus, the name by which he is known in many parts of the world today.

Philippines

The Christmas season in the Philippines lasts from December 16 to January 6, highlighted by a series of Christmas services, pageants, and festivals. Filipinos enjoy the Christmas music provided by brass bands, carolers, and church bells.

At night the streets are lit with garlands of star lanterns, some as big as 30 feet across, and strings of colored lights. People often make their own star lanterns of bamboo, trimmed with colored foil.

Some towns have Christmas pageants called *panunuluyan* on Christmas Eve. People costumed as Mary and Joseph knock on doors, looking for a place to stay. As they progress they are followed by others until the whole town follows them to the church, where the story of the birth of Christ is reenacted.

Mali
Sri Lanka
Upper Volta
Fiji

Denmark

Danes have made contributions to Christmas customs in other countries, including Hans Christian Andersen's stories, "The Fir Tree" and "The Little Match Girl," which are read and told in homes around the world. A Dane invented the Christmas seal, and the collecting of Christmas plates also began in Denmark.

But the jolliest tradition from Denmark is that of the Christmas *nisser,* little gnomes who assist the *Julemand* (Yule Man) in delivering presents. They are mischievous creatures, usually pictured as being dressed in red, and often bearded, though there are female *nisser* too. People used to set a bowl of rice pudding outside the door on Christmas Eve to please the resident *nisse* and ensure good luck.

Christmas Eve services are held in the afternoon. More people attend this service than any other during the year. Afterward everyone returns home for a festive Christmas Eve supper of rice pudding, which has an almond hidden inside. Whoever finds the almond wins a prize, perhaps a pink marzipan pig. Christmas dinner is usually roast goose, stuffed with apples and prunes and served with red cabbage. Dessert may be apple cake, smothered with whipped cream. Other Christmas treats are *klejner* (fried bowknot cookies), thin almond cakes, and *pebernøder* (round hard peppernuts). In the country, farmers treat the birds to a sheaf of wheat on a pole or tree, called a *juleneg.*

Finally, on Christmas Eve, the parents carefully light the candles on the Christmas tree, which is decorated with stiff paper hearts filled with candy, garlands of small Danish flags and tiny hearts, and white-frosted gingerbread. Then the whole family joins hands and dances around the tree, singing carols like "I Am So Glad on Christmas Eve."

Venezuela

Pesebres, or manger scenes, are the center of Venezuelan life from mid-December until February 2, *Candelaria.* The *pesebre* may be small enough for a tabletop or large enough to fill a room, with furniture covered with cloth representing mountains. Balsa wood figures represent local people from every walk of life. The holy family, with flowers and lights, is added on Christmas Eve.

In Caracas, young people have a roller skating party on one of the main streets from midnight on Christmas Eve until time for mass, about dawn. Christmas music and folk tunes are provided by guitars, *maracas* (gourd rattles), and harps.

A traditional and uniquely Venezuelan holiday dish is *hallacas,* meat and herb pie with a cornmeal crust, cooked in banana leaves.

On New Year's Day a *Paradura del Nino* may take place. The *Nino,* Infant, is captured by friends from the crib of some careless person's *pesebre.* The only way to retrieve him is to throw a party for the "kidnappers" and friends. The *paradura* party includes fireworks, a musical ensemble with maracas, violin, and guitar, and an elaborate ceremony for finding the *Nino* and returning him to his place.

England
Spain
Luxembourg
Spain

Japan

Only a small number of Japanese people are Christian and celebrate Christmas as a religious holiday. Many of those who do prepare elaborate Sunday school programs with singing and recitations. Others take the opportunity to serve the poor or sick.

Yet many Japanese people are familiar with the secular aspects of Christmas, and the buying and selling of Christmas gifts is an important part of Japanese business. Japanese versions of western carols are sung, and some families eat turkey instead of rice, fish, and bean cakes. A Japanese god, *Hoteiosho,* is believed to have eyes in the back of his head to observe children's behavior, and is pictured much like Santa Claus.

New Year's Day is a more important holiday, and pine branches, ropes of twisted rice straw, and tiny oranges decorate Japanese homes. Children participate in bands and kite-flying contests, and are given as gifts branches of trees hung with small gifts. Special ceremonies are held to drive away evil spirits, and families are drawn together even more at this time than at Christmas.

Cameroon

Christmas in Cameroon is a time that children enjoy. Schoolchildren have a month-long vacation in order to help with the peanut and coffee harvests. But they also have time to play. They may build their own little huts from clay and reeds.

On Christmas Eve people gather in an open place in the center of the village. They build a great log fire, and the church service follows. In some places people are learning to tell the Christmas story, adapting and using their own music and traditional folk tales—replacing the western carols they had learned from missionaries. This makes the service more meaningful to the people of Cameroon.

After church the people dance and sing around the fire, to the music of drums of different sizes.

U.S.S.R.
Hungary
Greece

Namibia

For many years the people of Namibia (once known as South-West Africa) have fought for their independence. During this painful time the Christian church has supported and comforted the people of the land. So Christmas is a very important time for Christians in Namibia.

The central ceremony is the Christmas Eve service, which lasts from midnight until sunrise. People come from all the villages for miles around. The singing of the choirs and Sunday school during the service is beautiful, but the most breathtaking moment in the dark night is seeing the lines of flaming torches and lanterns carried by people coming from all directions—but all going to one place—the church.

Madagascar

Christmas in Madagascar is a religious holiday, but it is also a time of community celebration.

Very few homes have Christmas trees, but there is always one in the church. On the morning of Christmas Eve, all the Sunday school children happily decorate their church's tree with angels, stars, and other delicate trims, all of which the young people have spent many evenings making from white paper.

At eight o'clock that evening everyone in the whole village, Christian and non-Christian alike, goes to the church for the Sunday school program. The children have spent weeks preparing songs, readings, and poetry recitations for the enthusiastic audience. They dance around the Christmas tree and receive a sack of brightly-wrapped Christmas candies before the program is finally over, about midnight.

On Christmas Day the families return to church before enjoying spicy duck, goose, or chicken, steaming rice, and fresh fruit salad.

Greenland
Iraq
Algeria
Spain

Greece

St. Nicholas, who is regarded chiefly as a bringer of gifts in Western Europe, is the object of serious devotion for Orthodox Greeks. Together with Christmas, his birthday on December 6 is an important religious festival.

On Christmas morning children visit neighbors singing *kalanda* (the origin of our word *carol*), accompanied by drum and triangle.

Roast pork is usually prepared for Christmas dinner. A *Christepsonio* (Christ bread) is also traditional. In places it is customary to insert a small olive branch, hung with dried fruit, in the middle of the loaf. After the meal it is placed on a shelf near the household icons, where it is kept until Epiphany, when it is finally eaten.

Other breads are made in a variety of shapes. In some places a bun is kept all year, nailed to the wall. Some Christmas breads are dedicated to cattle, hens, or sheep, and in one area the first slice cut from the bread is always given to the first poor person who passes by.

Brazil

The cities in Brazil are much influenced by European and American customs, and decorated shop windows and colored lights are not unusual. In the homes customs are more similar to those in other Latin countries.

Families spend the days before Christmas making *pesebres* or Nativity scenes. Figures of a variety of sizes may be collected in a single *pesebre,* and brightly colored sawdust is a characteristic base material. The Christ child is placed in his crib on Christmas Eve. From Christmas until Epiphany children move the Three Kings a little closer each day to the manger, symbolizing the journey to Bethlehem.

Before the midnight service on Christmas Eve, the *cena* (supper) is prepared and the table is set so that the holy family can eat if they visit during the mass. After mass people celebrate most of the night.

Sometime on Christmas Eve, when children are asleep, *Papa Noél* fills their shoes with gifts. He is said to enter through a window, as houses in sunny Brazil rarely have chimneys.

Ethiopia

Iran

Zaire

Italy

Sweden

Swedish households wake early on St. Lucy's Day, December 13, to the strains of the old Sicilian song "Santa Lucia" and to the sight of the family's Lucia Bride, the eldest daughter, wearing a crown of greenery and lighted candles. She brings coffee and saffron-flavored "Lucia cats" (buns) to all her family. The feast not only honors St. Lucia, an early Sicilian Christian martyr, but also celebrates the winter solstice and the return of the light to the long, dark winter days. In many places there is a community celebration as well, with each Lucia Bride selected from among many girls contending for the honor. Most Swedish homes have beautiful Christmas trees decorated with candles, Swedish flags, and glistening tinsel. One might also see miniature straw goats, a traditional Christmas symbol.

At noon on Christmas Eve, *Julafton,* some families participate in a ritual known as *"doppa i grytan,"* dropping bread into a pot of drippings and broth. Dinner, however, is usually an elaborate smorgasbord, including *lutfisk* (specially prepared cod, with white sauce), ham, and ending with rice pudding. An almond hidden inside predicts a wedding for whoever finds it!

A little elf called *Jultonisten* surprises everyone with gifts at Christmas. If any accident or mischief occurs in the weeks before Christmas, it is likely that he is responsible. To prevent such mishaps it is customary to set out a bowl of porridge for him on Christmas Eve.

Church on Christmas Day is usually an early morning service, with dozens of candles lighting the predawn darkness.

Switzerland

People in Switzerland may enjoy one of a variety of Christmas traditions, depending on the area in which they live and its people's ethnic background.

In the German and French parts of Switzerland, the children eagerly await the arrival of the *Christkindli,* the Christ child, who is dressed like a winged angel with a shining crown. It is the *Christkindli* who delivers gifts, candy, fruit, and nuts to the children—in some remote villages arriving in a reindeer-drawn sleigh.

In other parts of Switzerland, Father Christmas and his wife Lucy (recalling St. Lucy) distribute gifts. Elsewhere St. Nicholas, with his bishop's mitre and crosier, visits homes and schools to give candy and nuts.

But people in all parts of Switzerland customarily attend church on Christmas Day, even if they have to come by ski, sled, or horse-drawn sleigh. And under many a star-topped Christmas tree is a *crèche,* or Nativity scene, focusing on the infant Jesus in his cradle.

Hungary

Bulgaria

Finland

As in Scandinavian countries, people in Finland prepare for Christmas with cooking and baking. Christmas Eve supper includes boiled cod, potatoes, pork or ham, vegetables, and the customary rice pudding with an almond inside. What makes the meal unique is that it follows a visit to the sauna! On Christmas Eve, the Christmas tree may be decorated with paper flags and cornucopias filled with homemade candies, apples, gilded walnuts, and tinsel. The tree is kept until January 13, Canute's Day.

Ukko ("Old Christmas Man"), wearing a long mustache instead of a beard, brings gifts to the children. He may be accompanied by Christmas elves in quaint brown knee-breeches and red caps.

Early Christmas morning, when it is still dark, people throughout the countryside set off for the church in pony-drawn sleighs. They spend the rest of the day in feasting and visiting, wishing everyone a *"Hauskaa Joulna,"* "Happy Christmas."

Spain

Christmas Eve in Spain is called *Nochebuena,* the "Good Night." There is a carnival atmosphere, with singing and dancing to the music of guitars, castanets, and *maracas* (gourd rattles) in the brightly lit streets. The festivities are interrupted for midnight mass, but may go on afterward until morning.

Spanish homes do not usually contain Christmas trees, but most have an elaborate *nacimiento,* or Nativity scene, lighted with candles and ornamented with clay figures of shepherds, animals (bulls and donkeys are characteristic), and the holy family. A traditional feature of the Spanish *nacimiento* is a stream of water (made from glass or plastic) complete with fish, tortoises, and other water animals, where women kneel to do the family laundry.

Cena de Nochebuena ("Christmas Eve Supper") is eaten after the church service, and may consist of roast pork or lamb, red cabbage stuffed with onions, almond soup, baked pumpkin, sweet potatoes, and chestnuts. Traditional confections include marzipan and *turron* (almond nougat). On the fifth of January, *Dia de los Reyes,* children put out their shoes to be filled by the Three Kings and hay to be eaten by their camels!

U.S.S.R.
Malta
France
Ireland

France

One of the most charming customs in France is that of a *crèche,* or Nativity scene. Nearly every family has a collection of little handcrafted terra-cotta figures, called *santons,* which it lovingly displays each year. The *santons* include not only traditional biblical figures, but peasants and their wives, shopkeepers, laundry women, and other village characters.

In some parts of the country, Christmas puppet shows are customary. In Provence, there are moving Christmas services which have evolved from medieval dramas called "mystery plays." Beside the altar is a crib containing a doll representing the infant Jesus, surrounded by local people representing the holy family and angels, and by the choirs and drummers. Before Communion, a shepherd leads a ram pulling a decorated cart containing a lamb. Other villagers, dressed in provincial Arlesienne shepherds' costumes, approach the altar and offer the lamb to the Infant. Then the priest proceeds with Holy Communion. Some French carols also originated in miracle or mystery plays.

A popular holiday dessert is the *buche de Noel,* a frosted cake in the shape of a log, recalling the yule logs that were once burned in fireplaces. Other favorite Christmas dishes are goose, buckwheat cakes with sour cream, oysters, goose liver patè, and turkey with chestnuts. These are served at a traditional postmidnight mass repast called *le revèillon.*

Zaire

In Africa people never eat alone. Extended families live together, and the table is always set for friends. This is also true at Christmas.

Midnight mass on Christmas Eve is very important, and afterward there is dancing and singing. On Christmas Day the people eat a festive meal of chicken and rice.

The people of Zaire are generally content with a simple meal of *manioc* (cassava) seasoned with Spanish peppers, but whoever comes by may take part. Anyone is welcome in this hospitable country. Formerly this tradition of hospitality existed also in European countries. It is still maintained in Africa.

Turkey
U.S.S.R.
Senegal
South Africa

U. S. S. R.

Christmas customs have been changing in the Soviet Union. Father Frost, the Russian Santa Claus, is becoming a more popular figure. But St. Nicholas was at one time very important. Also, a white-robed young girl called *Kolyada* formerly traveled through the town in a sled at Christmas time, accompanied by carolers, who were given presents in return for singing *kolyadki*. *Kolyada* ("Christmas") and *kolyadki* "carols") are derived from the word *Kalendae*, the pagan winter festival celebrated in pre-Christian times.

But the favorite Christmas story in old Russia was surely the story of Baboushka (which means "grandmother"). Baboushka was an old woman who lived by herself in a little hut. One day in the coldest part of the cold Russian winter Baboushka was busy trying to finish her housework when she heard a knock at the door. There stood three strangers dressed in magnificent robes.

They told her they were following a star to a little town where a young child lay, but they had lost sight of the star. They asked Baboushka to show them the way to Bethlehem. But Baboushka was afraid of the awe-

some strangers, and she didn't want to abandon her warm cozy hut on such a snowy night to trek across the unknown wastes of Russia. Besides, she wanted to finish cleaning her house—perhaps she would have time to go the next day. The Three Kings wanted to be on their way, however, as Baboushka was left behind. Some stories say she intentionally told them the wrong way.

Whatever the cause, the legend tells us that the next morning Baboushka was filled with remorse and hurried after the Three Kings to find the Holy Infant. By now fresh snow had covered their tracks and she soon lost her way. To this day she wanders about the earth looking for the child Jesus on Christmas Eve, bringing gifts of toys and candy to every child she sees on her way to make amends for not helping the Three Kings. She is especially kind and loving to babies, hoping that one of them, at last, will be the Holy Babe himself. No wonder children in Russia eagerly await her arrival after they are asleep on Christmas Eve!

Canada
Mongolia
Japan
Tibet

Ecuador

At Christmas time in Ecuador everyone, even the llamas in their bells and colorful blankets, is dressed in special finery.

In a typical ranch a place in or near the entrance hall is set aside for the *pesebre* or Nativity scene. A picture of Bethlehem is painted on the blue paper lining which serves as sky in the *pesebre* box. Beads are made of sand, and lakes are represented by mirrors. Figures of the holy family, shepherds herding sheep, Indian children in traditional costume, burros, and llamas are customarily made of bread dough.

In some places Indians, in costumes decorated with feathers, pay a visit to a *hacienda* (estate) of their employer. Accompanied by a shepherd's pipe and Quechuan chants, they bring simple gifts like oranges, sugar cane, eggs, and wool to the figure of the Baby Jesus in his manger.

Afterwards there are gifts and a festive meal of lamb, baked potatoes, and brown-sugar bread for everyone. Usually there are leftovers for the Indians to take home in clay jars.

Ireland

One of the most beautiful traditions in Ireland is the lighting of a candle to show Mary and Joseph the way to Bethlehem on Christmas Eve. If there is a daughter named Mary in the family, she is given the privilege of striking the match and placing the candle on the windowsill. The table is set with a loaf of Irish Christmas bread and milk, and the door is left open for the holy family, or any other traveler far from home. In times of religious conflict the candle has also served as a welcome to any priest who might be looking for protection or a place to stay.

On December 26, St. Stephen's Day, it is still the custom for young people to hunt and catch a wren, and, singing carols, to take it from house to house in a willow cage. Where no real wren is available, a stuffed wren or one made of straw is used. In some places a special trip is made to carry the bird to the "Lord of the Manor," or local squire, singing

The wren, the wren!
The king of all birds!
On St. Stephen's Day,
he was caught in the furze!

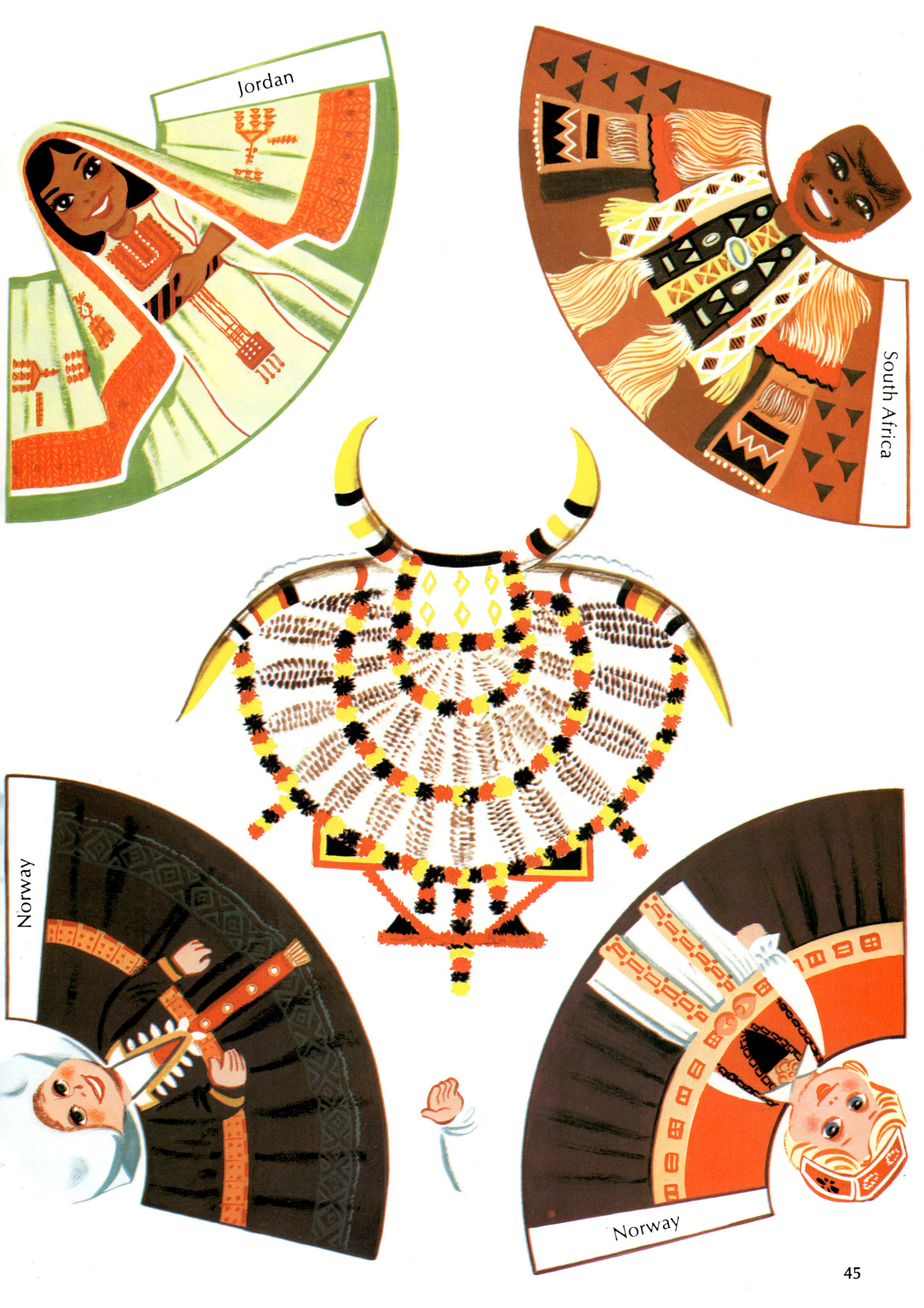
Jordan
South Africa
Norway
Norway

Canada

"Merry Christmas" and *"Joyeux Noel"* are both commonly heard in Canada at Christmas time. French and English traditions have both had their influence on Canadian customs, as have traditions from across the border in the United States.

In Quebec and other French-speaking parts of Canada, the custom of having crèches in homes and churches is common. In some churches the figures are clad in elaborately detailed garments, trimmed with silver or gilt. Churches are decorated with boughs of evergreens. People fast on Christmas Eve, perhaps having pea soup for supper.

After the Christmas Eve service there is a late supper called *le revèillon,* in which the fast is broken and everyone enjoys feasting and celebrating. *Père Noel* places gifts for the children in their shoes.

In the parts of Canada where the people are of English descent, turkey, mince pies, and plum pudding are popular. Children hang up their stockings, but the bewhiskered old gentleman who fills them may be called either Santa Claus or Father Christmas.

United States

The United States is remarkable for the rich variety of traditions from all over the world that have shaped Christmas. Almost every tradition found elsewhere in the world is represented in some part of the United States.

American cities, particularly large ones, are noted for their elaborate store windows and spectacular displays of colored lights. More than anywhere else in the world, homes are decorated outside as well as inside with images of Santa Claus and his reindeer, nutcrackers, even fairy-tale figures. Wreaths and sprays of evergreens, cascades of bells, or huge plaster snowmen may decorate front doors. Department stores and small specialty shops count on doing a large part of their business before Christmas.

But for many Americans Christmas is still centered in the family celebration of the birth of Jesus. Many families measure the weeks awaiting Christmas with an Advent wreath, churches are full on Christmas Eve, and candlelight services are very popular. Even families living in cities go often to tree farms together to find Christmas trees or yule logs. Many people not only display a Nativity scene in a place of honor, but make their own figures from baker's clay, balsa wood, batik, and needlepoint. Handcrafted tree decorations of straw, paper, metal, and many other materials hang on many trees, topped with the traditional star of Bethlehem. One lovely custom becoming more widespread is the use of *luminaria,* candles set up in sand-filled paper bags outside homes, churches, and even whole neighborhoods. Many Americans feel that by keeping their Christmas rituals and symbols simple they better fit the story of a Child born in poverty in a stable.

Portugal

Netherlands

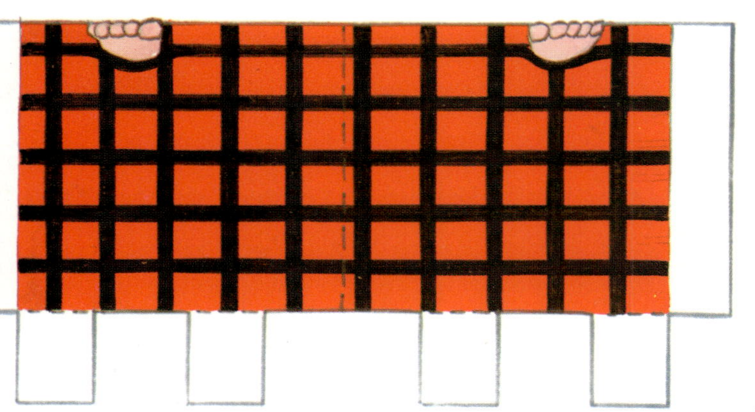

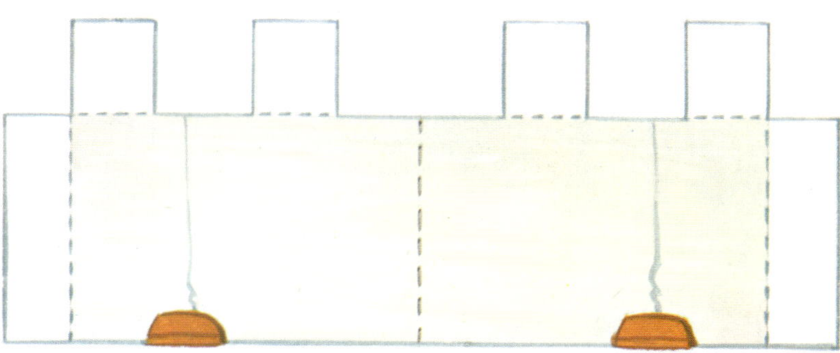

Jordan

Netherlands

Suggestions for use

1. You can arrange the figures in a spiral or star and place the crèche figures in the center. You may begin the first day of Advent with a few figures and add two or three each day until you add the infant Jesus in his manger on Christmas Eve.

2. Make your own *presepio* or *nacimiento* on a piece of cotton batting or foil. Add small trees, flowers, or small animals cut from magazines or catalogs, or drawn by hand, if desired.

3. For a more permanent arrangement, glue the figures to a piece of cardboard or lightweight plywood.
4. Glue the figures to a beach ball or large Styrofoam ball. Decorate with a bow and hang from the ceiling.

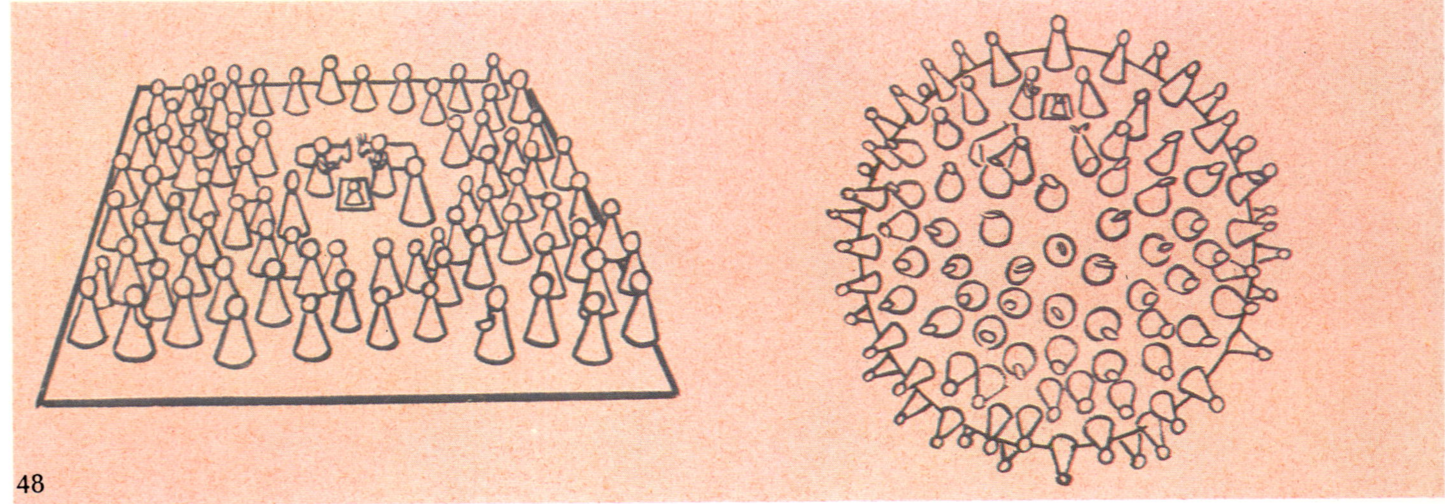